bubblegum heart
& other elastic things

poems written by

Quazaye Konkel

bubblegum heart & other elastic things

bubblegum heart & other elastic things

Dedicated to my first real love.

I'm grateful for our time together and all the lessons I learned along the way. Loving you was my greatest pride, my biggest passion, and a part of me will always wish things were different.

Also dedicated to the girl I was when I loved you, because she deserved a lot more.

bubblegum heart & other elastic things

Table of Contents

venus de milwaukee 1
vulnerable 2
kintsugi 3
always has been 4
yellow paint 5
do you ever feel like gum? 6
the crossing 7
consumed 8
bubblegum heart 9
monsoon season 10
groundwater 11
drowning lessons 12
jinx 13
she doesn't know 14
tulpa 15
one day 17
without you 18
delicate 19
empty 20
what stays 21
when I loved you 22
nightmares 24
for safekeeping 26

where it hurts	27
happy for you	28
never again	29
castor oil	30
monsters and thorns	31
suneater	32
seasons of loving	33

venus de milwaukee

i am soft beneath your hands

my skin dimples like marble
beneath your fingerprints
and suddenly
under the promise of the moon
i am Venus
and you are my sculptor -

i am s o f t b e n e a t h y o u r h a n d s

despite the hardness of my days
and art is all i have to be
until the sun rises again and bids me
return to stone
to face a world far too
harshly built for me -

i a m s o f t b e n e a t h y o u r h a n d s

and a r t is all i have to be

with you

vulnerable

it's peaceful in our bedroom
the air is lighter than
anywhere else;
maybe it's all the love we keep there -

all the kisses,
the touches,
the soft gasps, and
gentle sighs -

stored up like
nuclear winter is coming
to leave us cold
and empty and alone;

it drips off the walls like honey from a comb
and settles on the room like sweet perfume

where we love
and we live in love
every night that we say an *I love you*
that sounds more like a *goodnight*

where we finally rest in the embrace
of darkness and each other;
where we sin in the night
and are forgiven by morning;

we sleep and we talk and we laugh;
you whisper and I kiss you,
and we exist imperfectly together
fallible yet completely whole
in spite of completing each other.

kintsugi

bring to me your battered limbs,
your crushed spirit, your
splintered bones ;

give to me all your weary sighs,
your weathered hands, your
worn-out clothes ;

leave with me your heavy heart,
your tired mind, your
tattered soul ;

bring to me your broken things
and I'll repair their cracks
with gold .

always has been

It has been you, my dear, since
the time you made yourself laugh
and I first heard the sound that
would live in my heart forever.

It has been you, my sweet, since
the first night we shared a sky
and you touched my hand and
for the first time, I knew warmth.

It has been you, my darling, since
the very first fight we had when
I realized, for the very first time,
that I never wanted to lose you.

It has been you, my love --
Since the first of our firsts,
Until the last of my lasts –

It will always
be
you.

yellow paint

an artist
of me

we kiss,

you laugh,

we touch,

consume you

yellow paint

suddenly,

sunflowers

yellow vases

yellow tables

behind me.

a masterpiece.

i've never claimed to be

but you make one out

each time

each time

every.single.time

because i

like van gogh's

and

i am

in

on

and the blue is

suddenly I am

do you ever feel like gum?

I can still hear you laughing
as we watch the walls breathe,
the corners swirling like tiny wind storms
on the towering downtown ceiling

It was something I said, I asked,
"Do you ever feel like gum?"

The mint was fresh and cool in my mouth
strong like an army marching on my tastebuds,
like your hand as it held onto mine,
as they rested between us on the blankets

"Do you ever feel like gum?" I asked
I said it without thinking and I tried to explain

"Spritely and fresh, do you ever feel like gum?
Do you ever feel the way that gum tastes?
So good, so fresh, so clean
Do you ever feel pristine like that?"
Do you ever feel like gum?

You laughed some more
and I laughed with you
You have never felt like gum before,
and neither have I

Not until I met you.

the crossing

never before has
the swamp in my chest
felt so
        much like a meadow
        has
my mind been so sunny
        has
my heart felt so light
        has
that flower bloomed in my lungs

perhaps it was all that

        yellow paint.

consumed

some speak about love
as though it is a pyre
and hazard young things
to not be consumed

but if love is truly like
that of a raging fire
then i'd rather be burned
than choke on the fumes

and if love is truly something
upon which to choke
then rather than swallowed
it is caught in my throat

and if love truly is like
a sweet medication
then I'll take all of it
without hesitation

and if love truly is like
a sickness to death
then i'd rather be dead
than to have my health

but if love truly is nothing
but blazing fires and fumes,
than rather than burned,
i'd choose to be
consumed.

bubblegum heart

I know that I have you, but
sometimes I wish I had you
where *I want you*, because
for as much as **I love you**,
sometimes you take my
bubblegum heart
and chew it up
and spit it out.

monsoon season

what sense is there in loving deeply
if your beloved fears
leaving the shallows?

i fear holding back
the same way he fears
letting go

groundwater

i wish i could be
loved as deeply
as the well
in the bottom
of my chest
can
reach,
for as many
thirsty people
that drink
at the top,
hardly any
ever bother
to send the
bucket
back
down.

drowning lessons

      i hold on to you
      the way humans do
      to life rafts, a lifeline
      even when they know how to
           s w i m
      because they fear drowning
      more than they trust their
                                 own
                                         limbs.

jinx

I didn't mean to jinx it
when I asked if you were
okay…

I only meant
to kiss it
better.

she doesn't know

i know that i will be okay without you
it is my heart that i am
worried about

she doesn't know a world without you
she doesn't know
what is
coming

tulpa

I have always had a habit of overthinking.
I think, and I think, and I think until
a tulpa is dancing around the room like
it is praying for rain

And then, suddenly, we are worlds   apart
Just because I had a feeling that I had
to corner and put to bed; I had to know
I had to know --

This mess is somehow typical and yet
catastrophic in the sense that this time
your love is not reaching me when you disagree –
    Why isn't it reaching me?

I've been known to step on a landmine once
in a short while; some that I buried myself
(you know I can't read maps) and some that
you said are *fine*
                Why do you lie?

But this time I'm scared of being blown
to bits because this time, your love –
It is not reaching me, my love –
    Why isn't it reaching me??

I'm scared this time you will not
help collect the pieces once they're scattered
and I know better than to trust myself alone
because I know every stitch will be agony
~~without your hand in mine~~

(Even though I was right –
That something was wrong –
Because why would we fight
if nothing was wrong?)

And the tulpa laughs, it's been laughing for days
And I realize why it lingers here
It came for my blood, and it came for my bones,
and the rain that will cloud my eyes

        when I realize this

was the last time.

one day

maybe one day
it wont
take my breath away
or
burn a hole in my chest
or
make my stomach ache
or
make my mind race
to
take me back to the place
where
i was when you told me
on
my bedroom floor
gasping for breath
and
wanting to die
and
thinking, surely
dying would hurt less
than
the knife in my back
or
your voice in my ears
or
the punch to the gut
that
i wish you never told me
or
that the truth was not so
painful

without you

I feel like I'm in a million pieces
And the only one that knows my face is you

Like my life just stopped dead in its tracks and
Only you have the power to hit "resume"

I feel like I can't breathe without you, like
I don't know how to walk, can't sit, I can't think

Of a world where I exist without you - -
The thought of it alone has me on the brink

Of a primordial collapse, into a black hole
Where no bright lights can filter through

Because what is the point of all of this
If I have to do it all without *you*?

delicate

You handled me
like glass, and yet
here I am,
on the floor
in pieces at your feet --
wishing to be back
in your hands.

I guess they were
      too strong
for my delicate bones
or I was
      too fragile
to sip from forever,
and still –
I ache for your kiss
on my broken pieces.

because you loved me,
you loved me,
I was your favorite glass –
You drank from me
when you were thirsty
and cleaned the paint
from your brushes
on my lips;

and I loved you,
    I loved you -
with all my fragments,
    I love you -
with my jagged edges,
    I love you -
with my shattered design,
    I love you -
Can't you see that
    I still love you?

empty

i filled my day with things to do
and still i find myself missing you
your memory creeping in like ivy
along the red brick wall i built
around my mind

i filled my day with chores and plans
yet alone i sit, thinking of your hands
in my hands, my small hands, that
shake with withdrawal from the lack
of fingers between them

i filled my day with ideas and thoughts
but the inspiration was all for naught
because here you are, like the receipt
tucked between the pages of an old book
to mark my favorite spot

i filled my day with things and stuff
so the time that passed wouldn't be so rough
on my heart, or my head, or my hands,
or my soul, which feels heavier despite
losing half of itself

i filled my day today and yet
i still
feel
empty.

what stays

i have loved you
despite the odds,
despite myself,
in spite of gods
that wished us
a p a r t
every
day

i have loved you
through thunder,
through lightning,
through rain,
that threatened
to pour
and wash us
away

i have loved you
with bleeding parts,
with frozen lungs,
with a broken heart
to make it
all feel
okay

i have loved you
through many seasons,
regardless of weather,
and without reason
enough
to make you
want
to stay.

when I loved you

someone someday will read my poems
and realize how much you meant to me,
     how much I loved you,
and maybe my words will speak to them
the way that desperate hearts do
when they love another heart more
than they will ever love them back.

because loving you is heartbreak,
     because I will always loveyoumore,
and I'm afraid to share my words
     so no one will think ill of you

because I know that you aren't broken
but I also know that you don't feel thewayIdo,
     not fully,

and you'll never love me as much, as deeply,
as I love each freckle across the bridge of your nose
or every breath that you take when you are sleeping.

and I know you'll never love me as well
as I know the tenor of your longday voice
or the rise and fall of your chest when you're
     not-sleeping.

I am afraid to share my words so no one will think illofyou because I
know that you are not broken
and I know that you do love me
but I will always love you **more**.

so maybe one day you will read my poems
and realize how much I loved you.

…or perhaps one day you'll read my poems,
and wish I never had.

nightmares

i try not to think of you so often now
but there are pieces of us all around
the dime hanging from my keychain
your college hoodie on the ground

the sight of my own reflection haunts me
when i find the strength to get out of bed
because you always liked my hair like this
"the messier, the better," you always said

and i can't find the will to straighten it
so it doesn't remind me so much of you
can't find the energy, can't find the time
because i know you liked it pulled back, too

and then i'm a mess, i'm a total wreck
i love you too much for this to end
and i'm scared you're trying to move on   from me
cause i can't stand to lose my best friend

cause i can't stand to just let you go
i don't care what the saying is, i don't want to
there is too much love trapped in my chest
and when I bleed, i bleed for you

and i'm bleeding, i'm bleeding red
i'm so scared i'm bleeding out
because it just doesn't stop bleeding
when i have to go on without

you
i want *you*
i want you back
i want you *now*

my heart's an open wound
and you're all i think about

and i need you, *i miss you*
this space just doesn't feel right
when it's meant to be us, you and me,
against the world, against the night

so why am i alone in the dark
without your arms around me here?
why am i haunted in my sleep
before your ghost even appears?

i don't want this

i don't want this.

for safekeeping

i tore down the photos
on the walls in the room
where you lived in my heart

i changed the locks
so you couldn't walk right back in
when you want to come home...

then i remembered
this was never home to you.

if it was, you would not have left.

then i realize this is not home to me, either

only i cannot leave this place –

i must have locked myself in

when i was locking you out.

where it hurts

i tell myself i cannot live here
where it hurts to be but i hold on
because it still feels like
i'm close to you

i tell myself i cannot live here
in this mess, in this grave
where everything around me is
long dead and gone away

i tell myself i cannot live here
where it still feels like loving you
just because it is what i know

because you do not live here
with me anymore
and we both know
i could never stand to be

alone.

happy for you

and i'm happy for you…

the way that i was happy for
the dog i wanted to take home
who was adopted before
i could get there
despite
having an appointment,
an approved application,
a three hour drive,
and my heart set.

i'm happy for you
for finding your voice
and doing what is right
for you

but i'm so,
so
sad
for me.

never again

i know that i
must feel this

i must feel this
so i remember
never
to do this
to myself

again.

castor oil

heart break
tastes like castor oil
a catalyst for the
constipation of the brain
that being in love will give you.

it will go down easier if you don't resist

                                            just swallow it

and given the time to let it settle
you won't feel so weighed down when it
finally passes through you

monsters and thorns

i don't mean to
make monsters of men
especially not of
the man I loved,
the one I still love,
underneath these
bloody pages

it is just that this rose
is no longer in bloom
and all that is left
are the thorns.

suneater

I would still swallow the sun for you --
Just to give birth to the stars at night
So that you can see in the darkness
That you find yourself lost in lately.

I would make them constellations
Of the beautiful things we created
Of our time together, our memories
So that you might have some company.

I would fill them with my love for you
So that they shine as brightly as your eyes
When you're laughing at your own jokes
And I can't help but laugh along.

And I would fill them with my love for you
So that they burn as warm as your touch
On my skin, my moon-frozen skin,
In the dead of night, when it's just us.

And I would fill them with my love for you
Enough that they shine for you forever,
So even if you must take this journey alone
You never have to question again

If you are loved –
If you are worth loving –
If you are valued –
If you are *enough* –

Because I would swallow the sun for you
If it meant you could see in the dark.

seasons of loving

loving you has been summer ;
it's been bright and it's been free
it's also been so hot sometimes
i couldn't stand it touching me

loving you has been autumn ;
my favorite colors, my favorite space
but brimming with a nostalgia
that i can't exactly place

loving you has been winter ;
things have frozen and things have died
but you're the sweater that i slipped on
when it got too cold inside

loving you has been spring ;
full of fresh starts and promises kept
riddled still with knee-deep puddles
formed by the tears that i have wept

loving you has had its seasons
i've always known it would be true
but wind, sleet, rain, or shine –

i loved weathering it with you.

bubblegum heart & other elastic things

Thank you for reading.
-   q.k.

bubblegum heart & other elastic things

About the Author

A 20-something bi (racial, polar, sexual) writer from southeast Wisconsin finding her voice through writing poetry, fiction, and silly things in between.

She attended Marquette University where she graduated with an undergraduate degree in Writing Intensive English in 2019. She is currently attending Western Governors University where she's taking a stab at yet another kind of writing — JavaScript.

She lives with ADHD and Bipolar II, which she maintains is just depression with extra steps, but her "secret passengers" (as she calls them) do lend a lot to the creative process when they want to. Something something lemons, something something lemonade.

This is her first chapbook, and she's so grateful that you're here.

Happy healing.

bubblegum heart & other elastic things

Printed in the USA
CPSIA information can be obtained
at www.ICGtesting.com
LVHW011557120823
754934LV00014B/921